What about... AIDS?

Student Book

by Rodney L. Rathmann

Write to Library for the Blind, 1333 S. Kirkwood Road, St. Louis, MO 63122-7295 to obtain *What about AIDS?* (Student Book) in braille or sightsaving print for the visually impaired.

Scripture quotations in this publication are from The Holy Bible: NEW INTERNATIONAL VERSION, copyright © 1973, 1978, 1984 by the International Bible Society. Used by permission of Zondervan Bible Publishers.

What about...
AIDS?

Student Book

Writer: Rodney L. Rathmann
Editor: Arnold E. Schmidt
Consultant: Carl J. Moser

CONCORDIA.
PUBLISHING HOUSE
3558 SOUTH JEFFERSON AVENUE
SAINT LOUIS, MISSOURI 63118-3968

3

Meet Steve . . .

Seventeen-year-old Steve Dolber finally found the courage to look into the bathroom mirror, but the pale and withered face that stared back reminded him more of a death camp survivor than of himself.

During the past several months his tall and muscular frame has wasted away to a mere 87 pounds. These days he is often disoriented and has trouble remembering things. A former athlete, he now walks with a feeble shuffle. Soon he will die. Steve has AIDS.

What is AIDS and what has it done to Steve's healthy body?

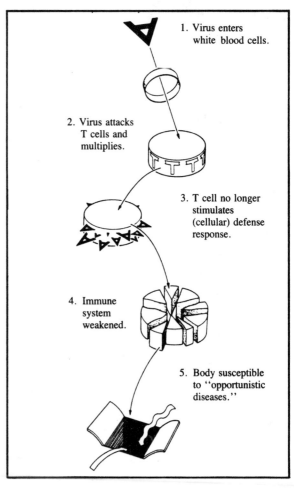

1. Virus enters white blood cells.

2. Virus attacks T cells and multiplies.

3. T cell no longer stimulates (cellular) defense response.

4. Immune system weakened.

5. Body susceptible to "opportunistic diseases."

AIDS stands for Acquired Immune Deficiency Syndrome. It is a relatively new disease. Its virus actually has three names, HIV, HTLV-III, and LAV. Like any virus, it passes from one person to another and causes illness.

When the AIDS virus enters someone's body, it makes itself a guest of the genetic material inside the white blood cells, or T cells, which help our bodies fight disease. Here it remains quietly within its host for months or even years, until another germ invades the body. When the white blood cells are called into action and begin to reproduce, the AIDS virus activates itself, mass reproduces, and kills the cell that has been its host. Thus, it makes the body's immune system defenseless against even the most minor of illnesses.

Once an individual has become infected with the AIDS virus, the disease can progress in different ways. Some people don't appear to be sick and may not come down with the disease for many years, if ever. But they may still pass the disease on to others. In other persons the symptoms develop early and the disease progresses rapidly.

– ARC –

Some infected persons have a few of the AIDS symptoms for a long period of time without being terminally ill. Doctors refer to this condition as ARC (AIDS Related Complex). The person with ARC usually suffers from anxiety and depression fearing that ARC will develop into AIDS.

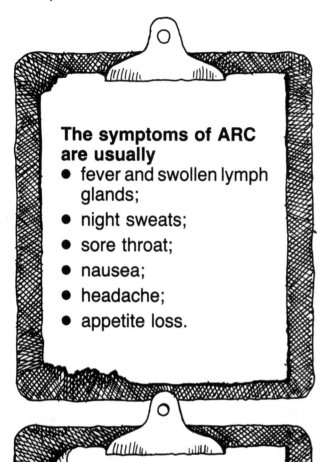

The symptoms of ARC are usually
- fever and swollen lymph glands;
- night sweats;
- sore throat;
- nausea;
- headache;
- appetite loss.

As the illness intensifies a more severe set of symptoms emerges including
- extreme enlargement of lymph nodes;
- weight loss;
- diarrhea;
- high fever;
- chronic fatigue.

The Disease Progresses

As the AIDS virus destroys the body's immune system, infections enter the body causing illnesses that could otherwise have been warded off.

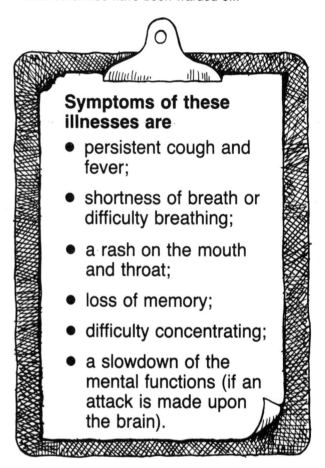

Symptoms of these illnesses are
- persistent cough and fever;
- shortness of breath or difficulty breathing;
- a rash on the mouth and throat;
- loss of memory;
- difficulty concentrating;
- a slowdown of the mental functions (if an attack is made upon the brain).

In the end the patient dies, not from AIDS as such, but from one of the illnesses the body was unable to fight off.

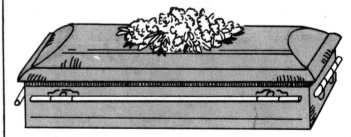

There is no cure for AIDS. Neither is there a vaccine to prevent it.

Searching God's Word . . . for Answers

Most (over 70%) of those with AIDS acquired it directly through some sinful action, such as homosexual sex, sex outside of marriage, or the abuse of intravenous drugs. Still Steve and others with AIDS wonder "Why?" or "Why me?" What answer to this question do you find in **Romans 5:12?**

How does God view sexual relations between persons of the same sex? See **1 Corinthians 6:9–10.**

Does God want people to die for their sinful acts so they can get what they deserve? See **Ezekiel 33:11.**

What is our Christian responsibility toward someone caught in sin according to **Galatians 6:1** and **Romans 10:17?**

Why can no one rightfully scorn or ridicule someone who has AIDS? See **Ecclesiastes 7:20.**

What condemnation (Law) and what Good News (Gospel) do you find in **Romans 6:23?**

What Good News do each of the following passages offer to all repentant sinners? **John 3:16; 1 John 1:7.**

Romans 5:12: Sin entered the world through one man, and death through sin, and in this way death came to all men, because all sinned.

1 Corinthians 6:9–10: Do you not know that the wicked will not inherit the kingdom of God? Do not be deceived: Neither the sexually immoral nor idolaters nor adulterers nor male prostitutes nor homosexual offenders . . . will enter the kingdom of God.

Ezekiel 33:11: Say to them, ''As surely as I live, declares the Sovereign Lord, I take no pleasure in the death of the wicked, but rather that they turn from their ways and live. Turn! Turn from your evil ways!''

Galatians 6:1: If someone is caught in a sin, you who are spiritual should restore him gently.

Romans 10:17: Faith comes from hearing the message, and the message is heard through the word of Christ.

Ecclesiastes 7:20: There is not a righteous man on earth who does what is right and never sins.

Romans 6:23: The wages of sin is death, but the gift of God is eternal life in Christ Jesus our Lord.

John 3:16: God so loved the world that He gave His one and only Son, that whoever believes in Him shall not perish but have eternal life.

1 John 1:7: The blood of Jesus, His Son, purifies us from all sin.

Meet Angie . . .

Angie was thinking about the latest heavy problem to settle upon her life when the junior high science teacher asked her to define *metamorphosis*. She hadn't read her assignment and didn't have a clue as to the word's meaning. But when the boy in the front defined metamorphosis as the drastic changing of an organism, Angie thought of herself.

Four years ago Angie was a different person. She was bright, happy, and well-adjusted. Then her family experienced the tragic car accident that took her baby brother's life. Angie had lost a great deal of blood and was kept in the hospital for a long time. Afterward her parents blamed each other for what happened. A year later they got a divorce. Angie felt like everything was her fault. She lost interest in schoolwork and friends.

Things went from bad to worse after her mother remarried. Her stepfather didn't like her, her mother seemed distant and pre-occupied, and her dad lived far away. Then Angie began to experiment with drugs and sex. School became a place to meet people who could provide her with both.

Now Angie has AIDS.

How does a person get AIDS and how can I avoid getting it?

Most people with the AIDS virus got it during sexual contact or through the sharing of needles when "shooting" drugs (injecting drugs with a hypodermic needle). AIDS can also be acquired from a transfusion of blood containing the virus. (Children born to mothers carrying the virus sometimes acquire AIDS from their mothers.)

Although the AIDS virus lives in several body fluids, it travels from one person to another in these three: blood, semen, and vaginal secretions. It usually enters the bloodstream through unseen tears in a person's rectum, vagina, or penis as the result of intercourse. Sometimes it enters a person's bloodstream directly via a contaminated needle.

AIDS CASES
How Acquired

70% Homosexual Activity

25% Drug Abuse

5% Other

Statistics compiled in 1987 show that about 70% of AIDS sufferers throughout the country are homosexual men who engage in anal intercourse. But AIDS does not spread only through homosexual practices. The virus can also be contracted through normal sexual intercourse. The risk of AIDS infection becomes greater as the number of persons with whom one has sexual intercourse increases.

Drug abusers who share needles are another group at high risk of becoming infected by the AIDS virus. This groups represents about 25% of the AIDS cases in the country. The AIDS virus in contaminated blood is left in the needle, syringe, or any other apparatus used to insert drugs. When drug users share their equipment, the virus is transferred into another person's bloodstream.

A very small percentage of persons in the U.S. has contracted AIDS through contaminated blood that they received during a blood transfusion or from blood products that help blood to clot.

Currently blood donors are screened. Blood that has been collected for use is tested for the presence of the AIDS virus, and blood containing it is destroyed.

According to a 1987 report from the U.S. Public Health Service, approximately one-third of the babies born to AIDS-infected mothers become infected with the AIDS virus.

How can I avoid getting AIDS?

The AIDS virus dies very quickly in the air, and there are no known cases of someone acquiring AIDS from casual contact. There is no evidence that you can get AIDS from a toilet seat or that AIDS can spread from one person to another through the sharing of food, cups, or toothbrushes. Neither can a person get AIDS by hugging or kissing. Research also indicates that you cannot get AIDS from insects such as mosquitoes, or from dogs, cats, or other pets. AIDS finds a new host when the blood, semen, or vaginal fluids of an infected person enter the bloodstream of another.

In order to offer some safety precaution against AIDS, public health officials recommend using condoms during sexual intercourse. This recommendation promotes the breaking of God's laws regarding the use of His gift of sex. Furthermore, condoms do not offer 100% protection against AIDS. Neither do they guarantee 100% protection against pregnancy.

Angie could have acquired AIDS in three ways. Name them.

Two of these ways are sins against the Fifth and Sixth Commandments. Society today seems to encourage these sins. Pornography and drug use are on the rise. Television and movies regularly portray sexual intercourse as something to be expected between a man and woman who are attracted to each other. Some accept homosexuality as an alternative lifestyle.

JUST SAY NO!

Looking to God's Word
. . . for Answers

Angie could have received the AIDS virus from the blood transfusion she received after the car accident. Most likely, though, it entered her body as the direct result or her sins against the Fifth and Sixth Commandments. God condemns these sins together with all others. But for what purpose? See **John 3:17.**

What does God want for Angie? See **1 Timothy 2:4.**

According to **Ezekiel 33:7–9,** what is our Christian duty toward Angie if she is unrepentant of her sinful lifestyle?

What promise of Jesus exists for all who repent of their sin? See **2 Corinthians 5:21; Isaiah 53:5;** and **John 8:36.**

Angie fell into a sinful pattern because she was looking for love and acceptance. But Angie and others like her quickly discover that drugs and sex do not provide what is missing in a person's life. Instead, they bring with them new problems and greater pain.

How could the words of **John 6:37** have had special meaning for Angie when she felt like no one cared? See **John 15:13.** How has Jesus made Himself our best friend? What additional promise has our friend given us in **Matthew 28:20b?**

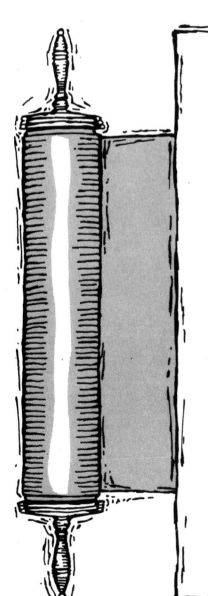
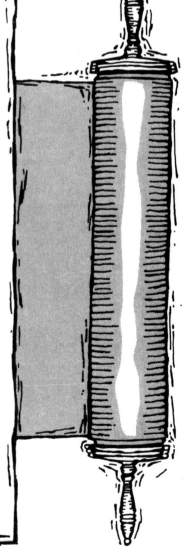

John 3:17: God did not send His Son into the world to condemn the world, but to save the world through Him.

1 Timothy 2:4: [God] wants all men to be saved and to come to a knowledge of the truth.

Ezekiel 33:7–9: I have made you a watchman for the house of Israel; so hear the word I speak and give them warning from Me. When I say to the wicked, ''O wicked man, you will surely die,'' and you do not speak out to dissuade him from his ways, that wicked man will die for his sin, and I will hold you accountable for his blood. But if you do warn the wicked man to turn from his ways and he does not do so, he will die for his sin, but you will have saved yourself.''

2 Corinthians 5:21: God made Him who had no sin to be sin for us, so that in Him we might become the righteousness of God.

Isaiah 53:5: But He was pierced for our transgressions, He was crushed for our iniquities; the punishment that brought us peace was upon Him, and by His wounds we are healed.

John 8:36: So if the Son sets you free, you will be free indeed.

John 6:37: Whoever comes to Me I will never drive away.

John 15:13: Greater love has no one than this, that he lay down his life for his friends.

Matthew 28:20b: I am with you always, to the very end of the age.

The message on the granite slab was brief and to the point:

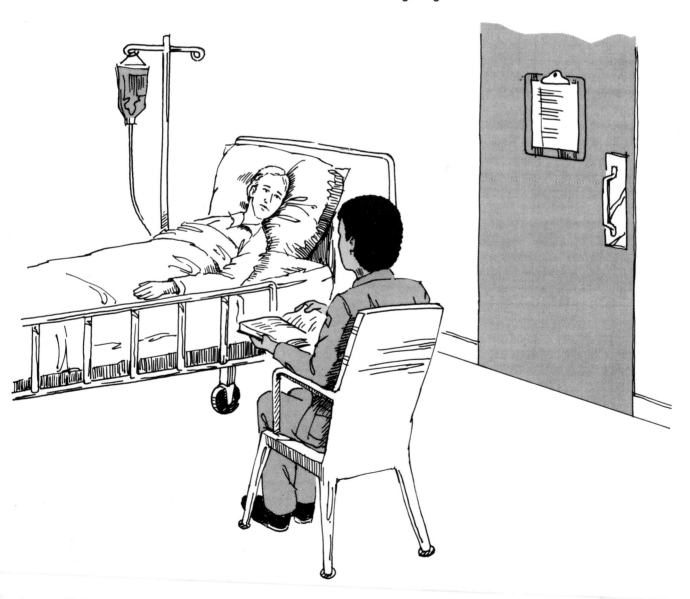

Andrew Dahlenbach
Born: August 27, 1965
Died: September 14, 1987

Andy didn't live long after he found out he had AIDS. But he suffered much during this time with a misery that extended beyond the physical suffering and loneliness brought on by the disease. Andy suffered deeply from guilt. At first no one came to visit him.

Then a nurse, whose capacity for care and kindness extended beyond the obligations of her job, contacted the pastor from Andy's hometown. The pastor in turn called Bill, a former classmate of Andy, who lived nearby. Bill (who was not a homosexual) came to see Andy in the hospital and remained with him during the final, painful days.

Andy was fortunate to have a friend like Bill. Bill reminded Andy of God's love and promises, read to him from the Bible, and prayed with him. Andy confessed his sins, and Bill assured him that they were all forgiven. Jesus had given His life long before to pay for all of Andy's sins, including those that had resulted in his getting AIDS.

When Jesus spoke the Sermon on the Mount, He talked about love. Jesus told His listeners to love even their enemies **(Matthew 5:44)** and to let the light of their faith shine to those around them **(Matthew 5:16).**

In **John 15:12–13** Jesus commands His followers of all time, "Love each other as I have loved you." And speaking of His crucifixion He added, "Greater love has no one than this, that he lay down his life for his friends."

Why do you suppose Bill reached out to Andy and loved and cared for him even though Andy had been living in sin? See **Ezekiel 33:11.**

Where did Bill find the motivation to love others as he did? See **Ephesians 3:20.**

What do you suppose Bill's friends or the members of his family may have thought when they learned that Bill was spending time with a homosexual?

When the religious leaders of Jesus' day noticed that He was socializing with sinners, Jesus let them know that He had come not for those who thought they had no sin, but for those who needed to hear the Gospel **(Matthew 9:9–12).** How do you suppose Bill responded to questioning friends and family members?

Perhaps after Andy died his family and friends felt guilty that they had not gone to be with him in the hospital. What comfort do the words of **2 Corinthians 7:9–10** offer these people as they come to God with their own sin? As they remember Andy?

Homosexual behavior is sinful. The Bible speaks out clearly against it in **Romans 1:26–32.** If Andy had been unrepentant, perhaps Bill would have quoted to him from **Galatians 6:7–8** which says, "Do not be deceived: God cannot be mocked. A man reaps what he sows. The one who sows to please his sinful nature, from that nature will reap destruction." How do these words apply to Andy's situation?

We don't know what Bible passages Bill read to Andy. He may have read the following. How would each be meaningful to Andy? **Isaiah 1:18; Psalm 103:1, 3, 12; 1 John 1:7; 1 Peter 1:3–9; Colossians 3:13.**

God's Words for Us . . .

- Ezekiel 33:11: "Say to them, 'As surely as I live, declares the Sovereign Lord, I take no pleasure in the death of the wicked, but rather that they turn from their wicked ways and live. Turn! Turn from your evil ways! Why will you die, O house of Israel?'"

- Ephesians 3:20: Now to Him who is able to do immeasurably more than all we ask or imagine, according to His power that is at work within us, to Him be glory in the Church and in Christ Jesus throughout all generations, for ever and ever! Amen.

- Matthew 9:9–12: As Jesus went on from there, He saw a man named Matthew sitting at the tax collector's booth. "Follow Me," He told him, and Matthew got up and followed Him. While Jesus was having dinner at Matthew's house, many tax collectors and "sinners" came and ate with Him and His disciples. When the Pharisees saw this, they asked His disciples,

  "Why does your Teacher eat with tax collectors and 'sinners'?" On hearing this, Jesus said, "It is not the healthy who need a doctor, but the sick. But go and learn what this means: 'I desire mercy, not sacrifice.' For I have not come to call the righteous, but sinners."

- 2 Corinthians 7:9–10: Now I am happy, not because you were made sorry, but because your sorrow led you to repentance. For you became sorrowful as God intended. . . . Godly sorrow brings repentance that leads to salvation and leaves no regret.

- Romans 1:26–32: Even their women exchanged natural relations for unnatural ones. In the same way the men also abandoned natural relations with women and were inflamed with lust for one another. Men committed indecent acts with other men, and received in themselves the due penalty for their perversion. Furthermore, since they did not think it worthwhile to retain the knowledge of God, He gave them over to a depraved mind, to do what ought not to be done. They have become filled with every kind of wickedness, evil, greed and depravity. They are full of envy, murder, strife, deceit and malice. They are gossips, slanderers, God-haters, insolent, arrogant and boastful; they invent ways of doing evil; they disobey their parents; they are senseless, faithless, heartless, ruthless. Although they know God's righteous decree that those who do such things deserve death, they not only continue to do these very things but also approve of those who practice them.

- Isaiah 1:18: Though your sins are like scarlet, they shall be as white as snow.

- Psalm 103:1, 3, 12: Praise the Lord, O my soul; all my inmost being, praise His holy name . . . who forgives all your sins and heals all your diseases . . . as far as the east is from the west, so far has He removed our transgressions from us.

- 1 John 1:7: But if we walk in the light, as He is in the light, we have fellowship with one another, and the blood of Jesus, His Son, purifies us from all sin.

- 1 Peter 1:3–9: Praise be to the God and Father of our Lord Jesus Christ! In His great mercy He has given us new birth into a living hope through the resurrection of Jesus Christ from the dead, and into an inheritance that can never perish, spoil or fade—kept in heaven for you, who through faith are shielded by God's power until the coming of the salvation that is ready to be revealed in the last time. In this you greatly rejoice, though now for a little while you may have had to suffer grief in all kinds of trials. These have come so that your faith—of greater worth than gold, which perishes even though refined by fire—may be proved genuine and may result in praise, glory and honor when Jesus Christ is revealed. Though you have not seen Him, you love Him; and even though you do not see Him now, you believe in Him and are filled with an inexpressible and glorious joy, for you are receiving the goal of your faith, the salvation of your souls.

- Colossians 3:13: Bear with each other and forgive whatever grievances you may have against one another. Forgive as the Lord forgave you.

- Romans 8:28: We know that in all things God works for the good of those who love Him, who have been called according to His purpose.

- 2 Corinthians 12:9: My grace is sufficient for you, for My power is made perfect in weakness.

  1 Corinthians 10:13: But when you are tempted, He will also provide a way out so that you can stand up under it.

Every AIDS sufferer needs Christian friends like Bill. Following is a list of things you can do to share the love of Christ with a person who has AIDS and the members of his or her family.

Things to do . . .

- Be a friend. Listen. AIDS sufferers feel lonely and rejected.
- Do social things with persons with AIDS. Study God's Word with them. Take them to church and Sunday school with you. Let them know you care.
- Talk about sin, God's love, Jesus' suffering and death, and the free gift of eternal life. Endless pain and misery in hell is far worse than AIDS.
- Pray for and with AIDS sufferers and their families.

- Provide family members with a break. Take over at the bedside of the AIDS sufferer for an hour or two.
- Be an ear for the members of the AIDS sufferer's family. Run errands and do chores. *Do* for them.

Not everyone who has AIDS received it through sinful sexual activities or drug abuse. Some have gotten AIDS as victims of rape, from sexual contact with an unfaithful spouse, from a transfusion of AIDS-contaminated blood, or from mothers with AIDS. What comfort does God offer these believers in the words of the following passages: **Romans 8:28; 2 Corinthians 12:9; and 1 Corinthians 10:13?**

Ask Pat

Advice for the Young Christian Reader

Dear Pat,

I am normal. At least I think I am. I am active in the youth group at church, do okay in school—most of the time, and take part in a number of extracurricular activities. I have lots of friends.

Now about my problem. Some kids in my neighborhood tease me, calling me names like *goody-goody* and *holy one* because I don't do drugs or have sex. They are really getting me upset. Though I try not to let on that their comments bother me, they do. Sometimes I think I should just go along with them and have sex. After all, I know God loves me, and that He will forgive me. I feel frustrated and "out of it." What should I do? Can you help me?

Pure Agony

God wants His children to enjoy life to the fullest **(John 10:10b).** But He also wants us to honor Him by following His will in the way we use His gifts. After all, He has our best interests at heart.

God has reserved sexual intercourse as a special union between man and woman to be enjoyed only in marriage. (See **Mark 10:6–9.**) We live in a world filled with temptations. Like the author of the letter above, many young persons struggle to lead a sexually pure and decent life. Where can we go for help with this problem? God directs us to His Holy Word.

The apostle Paul writes about sexuality in a letter to the people of Ephesus, **But among you there must not be even a hint of sexual immorality, or of any kind of impurity, or of greed, because these are improper for God's holy people (Ephesians 5:3).** What similar advice does Paul give Timothy in **2 Timothy 2:22?** What special honor is given to the body of every believer **(1 Corinthians 6:19)?**

Where can we go for the strength to keep ourselves pure? See **2 Timothy 1:7.**

The temptation for young people to have sex outside marriage is nothing new. Long before the time of Jesus, a faithful follower of God named Joseph found himself living in the land of Egypt without the support and encouragement of God-fearing family and friends. The Egyptians, who did not worship the true God, had rather loose moral standards, and the wife of Joseph's master tempted him to have sex with her. But Joseph, no doubt remembering God's steadfast love, asked himself the question believers often ask themselves when resisting the temptation to sin, **How then could I do such a wicked thing and sin against God (Genesis 39:9)?**

Because Joseph obeyed God and refused to sin with his master's wife, he suffered wrongful accusation and landed in prison. Yet God took care of Joseph and eventually made him second in command over all the land of Egypt. Through him God saved Joseph's entire family from death by starvation. Besides God's steadfast love, what else can God's people remember when they suffer because of their faith **(Romans 8:18)?**

What is the source of power for God's people when they face the challenge of obeying God in a disobedient world **(1 Peter 1:5; 1 Corinthians 1:8)?** Jesus is God; He is holy. How can He understand our temptations and struggles to obey **(Hebrews 2:18)?**

How about when we fail in our struggle to keep ourselves free from sins against the Sixth Commandment—what then? See **Acts 3:19.**

In addition to obeying God's commands and avoiding the possibility of getting AIDS, what are some other benefits that exist in saving sex for marriage?

Reviewing God's Word

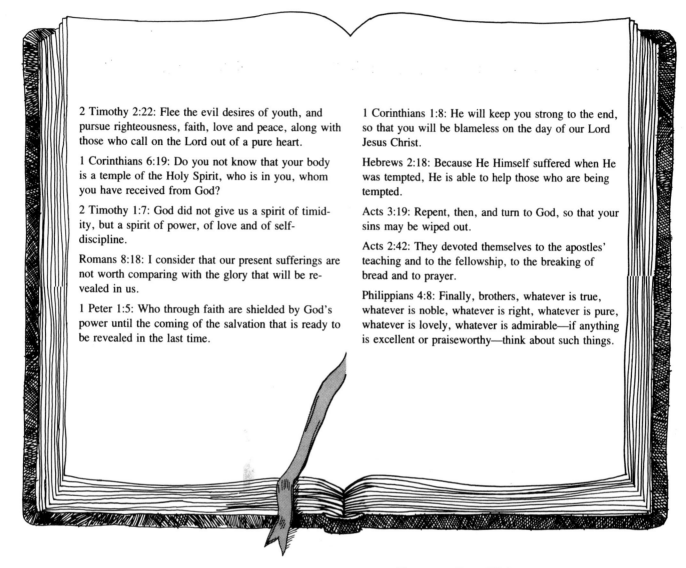

2 Timothy 2:22: Flee the evil desires of youth, and pursue righteousness, faith, love and peace, along with those who call on the Lord out of a pure heart.

1 Corinthians 6:19: Do you not know that your body is a temple of the Holy Spirit, who is in you, whom you have received from God?

2 Timothy 1:7: God did not give us a spirit of timidity, but a spirit of power, of love and of self-discipline.

Romans 8:18: I consider that our present sufferings are not worth comparing with the glory that will be revealed in us.

1 Peter 1:5: Who through faith are shielded by God's power until the coming of the salvation that is ready to be revealed in the last time.

1 Corinthians 1:8: He will keep you strong to the end, so that you will be blameless on the day of our Lord Jesus Christ.

Hebrews 2:18: Because He Himself suffered when He was tempted, He is able to help those who are being tempted.

Acts 3:19: Repent, then, and turn to God, so that your sins may be wiped out.

Acts 2:42: They devoted themselves to the apostles' teaching and to the fellowship, to the breaking of bread and to prayer.

Philippians 4:8: Finally, brothers, whatever is true, whatever is noble, whatever is right, whatever is pure, whatever is lovely, whatever is admirable—if anything is excellent or praiseworthy—think about such things.

So often Christian people feel they are all alone. Feeling alone in obedience to God is not new either. The prophet Elijah once told God that he was the only one left in all of Israel that had not rejected Him. But Elijah was mistaken. God told him there were 7,000 in Israel who remained faithful.

The children of God are never alone. And we find renewed strength when we join forces with one another. Our Lord has promised, **"Where two or three come together in My name, there am I with them" (Matthew 18:20).** What practical advice for building one another up in the faith do you find in **Acts 2:42?** in **Philippians 4:8?** What can the church do to help those who struggle with the problems and challenges of being a teenager?

You are Pat. Write your answer to "Pure Agony."

Printed in U.S.A.

20-2190
ISBN 0-570-09277-9